www.finishinglinepress.com

Beyond the Noisy Membrane

poems by

Mary Imo-Stike

Finishing Line Press
Georgetown, Kentucky

Beyond the Noisy Membrane

ACKNOWLEDGMENTS

The following poems have appeared in these journals or on-line journals. Some were earlier versions of what is here:

My Moon (as Wolf Moon), The Intruder, Bury Me Face Down in Spring, Why I Pick Up Rocks and Dreaming of Water, *Anthology of Appalachian Writers*
Iron Patty and The Man in the Theater, *Connotation Press*
I Found Honeysuckle, *Mountain Ink*
Perfect Kernel, *A Room of Her Own* Anthology
Beyond the Noisy Membrane, *Vandalia*
Down Poplar Fork, *Pikeville Review*
I rhyme//To see myself, to set the darkness, *Feed*
Young Crow, *K'in*

Special love and gratitude to the good friends who have supported me in this work, from outside the lit-academia arena, especially Monica Adams, Diane Shur, Mark Severs, Zena McFadden, and my sister Catherine Imo.

Publisher: Leah Huete de Maines
Editor: Christen Kincaid
Cover Art: Kimberly Hamill Dresch, Photographer and Artist
Author Photo: Kimberly Hamill Dresch, Photographer and Artist
Cover Design: Elizabeth Maines McCleavy

Order online: www.finishinglinepress.com
also available on amazon.com

Author inquiries and mail orders:
Finishing Line Press
PO Box 1626
Georgetown, Kentucky 40324
USA

Contents

My Moon

I'm in the family car
riding home from Grandma's,
through the city, before the expressway was born.
I am three years old, alone in the backseat.
I watch the moon out the car window.
It keeps its distance,
no matter how fast Dad drives
and it sees me, speaks to me

>more than the huge Coca-Cola sign,
>on the bottling plant we pass on Clinton Avenue,
>that vies to be a minor moon tonight—
>round too, but man-made,
>its red and white
>loud neon lights
>fill its circle line by line
>to outline its message "Drink Coca-Cola"
>until it's full of itself,
>then empties and starts once again.

But the white moon
with its full and floating face
declares its existence to me
not friendly or scary
just there,
filling up the sky.

I know
if I see it,
and listen to its vast and silent howl
I am here, too.

Iron Patty

Patty Kuhn, who had polio, in my first-grade class
wore braces on both legs
half-crutches with clamps holding her forearms,
enabling her to scuttle
across the oakwood classroom floor.
Her left hand, two fingers fused together,
a crooked, misshaped nail on her index finger.

We lined up one day two by two
on the way to the auditorium,
Patty assigned as my partner.
Standing in the hallway
and told to hold our partner's hand,
she reached out with a smile.
I hesitated, staring at her hand with the deformed fingers.
"Don't be afraid", Patty said, "it won't hurt you".
My cheeks burned.
I wanted to have a different partner,
hold hands with another girl, any other girl,
even Carol Mason, who everyone said had cooties.

I knew then I could not hide.
She saw what I was
with all my fears.
She was the girl in the iron lung,
who learned to write
with her pencil in her mouth,
the dirty, skinny waif with full moon eyes
behind the barbed wire fence in the concentration camps
we saw on TV;
the sick and starving child on the poster
of the Maryknoll missionaries in China.
She was all of them
who Mom said I was so lucky not to be.

And Iron Patty knew it,
she knew me.

Bottom Land

This bottom land where our house sits
was once an ancient river's bed,
flat in a land of mountains,
made by the delicious push
and leaden mass
of water.

Our garden, behind the house, gives up
rounded rock,
miniature manatees I want to nuzzle
then release back to their silent nests of soil.
Some imitate the tiny moons of planted planets
with fine tawny mineral lines,
strands of ochre, rusty amber,
and verdigris entwined with red coral,
spidering across their circumferences.

In my dreams
I reach into this base beneath my feet,
knead aside the round brown rolls
of molasses colored soil,
grasp and pull up
ginger-orange painted pottery pieces
I myself discarded centuries ago.

I Found Honeysuckle
To John

alongside the creek and clipped some
to bring home knowing you'd disapprove,
not take to the wildness that drew me to it.
But I knew that by the time it rooted,
sprouted fine pale hairs that tangled
in the water of a glass measuring cup
you'd have forgotten your doubts,
and by the time my vision of it coming to life
to cover the side of the garage on the white trellis
reaching for the gutter
and the powerful syrup sweet scent
teased your nose hairs
every time you mowed the lawn
burst into being
you'd love it as you love me
thinking it was your idea.

The Intruder

A small hank of grey fur
shows up in the evening
and meanders across the patio:
points of pink onionskin ear flesh
and long pink tail.

The rat worries my husband,
wakes him from post-supper stupor.
He talks of traps, my man,
the have-a-heart we used for flying squirrels,
now put away in the garage or barn attic,
too inconvenient to search for.

Our visitor reminds me
of the perils about to fall upon us:
financial devastation,
decimation of the environment
begun with the blasting away of our mountaintops,
and the growing probability of
poison water in our pipes.

The small grey and pink intruder
is gone for the night.
Tomorrow my husband will check his trap,
carefully bait and place it behind the porch rocker.
And we will buy
a shallow respite from danger.

On a Train

The young woman next to me on the train was knitting a dress on size 4 needles. Though of yarn, it was lacy, a sea foam green meant to hug her slender perfect rise from hips to chest and curve carefully around her peach-like breasts. Below it would cling and hug to 3 inches above her knees, the foam outlining the advance of her muscular thighs as she steps deliberately onto the stage of her world of Charlottesville, Virginia in this twenty-first century.

I lean back in my seat and think of the chunky scarf I knit as a teenager for my boyfriend in the cold country winters. On size 10 needles, it was long enough to circle his neck twice then fall proudly down his muscled back on top of his wine-colored wool winter jacket. It was striped, maroon and white, bright colors that stood for the boldness of my claim on him.

Though made years and miles apart, each garment knit from a sexy place, the raw and hopeful seed of feminine desire blossoming into outward garlands of bold expression.

The Man in the Theater

Is a stranger in his seventies, sitting on my left,
who I imagine is from a Western state,
someplace with a wide middle and big sky,
a windy place where topsoil is only borrowed
then passed on to the next county,
more suitable for ranching than farming.
The sleeve of his broad cloth shirt,
unbuttoned two from the collar
makes up the spare boundary between our arms
on our shared armrest.
The baggy drape of his khaki pants
keeps him at an appropriate space
from my bare crossed legs.

Even in silence, he exudes a steadfastness
tightly woven with gloom,
as if the wide and hungry thighs of his plain terrain
gave birth to the tedium he is doomed to carry.

Before long
I want to crawl into his skin
and try him on.
Break him open,
give him joy.

Bury Me Face Down in Spring

And I'll embrace this earth
        that holds the remains of my ancestors
        who pushed seed deep with bony fingers
        and painted their gibbous moon faces
        with streaks of reddish ochre
        and daubs of umber.
Bury me haphazardly,
        kicked in a pit like the Tollund Man,
        accused and spat upon
        in my coarse cloth coat
        with buttons I've carved from stones.
Bury me with your noose still wringing my neck
        so I will feel my brothers
        who hung as strange fruit
        overripe and clabbered in their innocence.
Bury me in my simple life,
        reading, loving, breathing
        like the pagans of Pompeii
        snuffed out like a candle flame
        against god's thumb and forefinger,
        quick and gone, under centuries of ash.

Perfect Kernel

On the house roof,
the mild November wind
blows my hair as fine as spider's breath
across my face
and I find on the rough grey
shingles' surface,
a perfect kernel of bright yellow corn.
I know my spirit sister visits me,
watches me
and leaves her golden gift
of sustenance and care.

Above, a crow,
in ascendance in his own web
that takes in our garden,
scavenged stalks cut down low
to straw-colored mounds,
the small outline of my house
and this ever-changing stretch of our sky.

And me, the girl on the roof,
stringing Christmas lights,
breathing in
my own small piece of it.

Beyond the Noisy Membrane

I have a new desire to move
into an outbuilding along the Interstate,
a natural gas field station,
where pipes connect and bury their way
into the dry stony ground.
How long before they'd find me? Put me away,
past my husband's hurt eyes, the neighbors saying,
"We didn't know she had a problem."

But before that I could stop asking permission
and just do what I could:
stay warm, eat plants, and contemplate
the constellations. Watch the hawk
I know patrols the hillside and the empty
cleared out lots that are a subdivision
that never happened.
Sleep just beyond the noisy membrane
of the rushing cars and semis.

Past the well-trimmed yards
and steamy asphalt driveways,
I will chew chicory leaves,
lean up against my cardboard headboard,
write my own new unsanctioned history.
I will see how the animals do it,
plan for the next darkness.

Down Poplar Fork

This morning I encounter
fresh roadkill,
squirrels, mostly,
dreamily on their backs,
legs splayed wide;
a child's stuffed duck,
forgotten and trampled
one wing flapping hopefully
against the rush of cars.

The remains of a whitetail doe
from last fall
have been rendered
into a pile of bright bleached residue
along the straight stretch
of Poplar Fork Road.
I never want to look at her,
but am compelled to do so.
I want to pluck out her skull
and keep in on my desk,
a place of honor.

I will tell stories about how she,
now an outline of streaked, blanched bone,
ran the woods,
slept in a grass-matted circle
and wore a naked necklace
of babies' breath and bats' teeth
in the dappled, herringboned sunlight.

Why I Pick Up Rocks

The quickening and rush to pluck
put my hands on
use a careful sideways rub
with my thumb across the mud-caked surface
to wipe away the clinging clay.

Smooth ovoids
orangey faces beneath their mud masks:
hallowed eyes and a smudge of mouth,
slash of brow lines,
lips painted by a line of mineral trace.

I have an affinity
with what's in the ground
cold and safe
sometimes forgotten
still here with us.
They wait beneath our footsteps
They hold our stories,
broken and discarded pieces
of our lives,
tin thimbles, glass bottles, bone buttons,
a doll's plastic hand
and the rocks the earth made.
They are patient in their limbo.

I pull them free, saying,
Tell me.

Dreaming of Water

This water I see in West Virginia,
an orange tailings-tainted pool
connects me to my father.

    He stands on the shore of Lake Ontario
    five hundred miles away
    and sings to me
    about the South-North flow of rivers,
    a rarity, like the Nile, like the New
    like the Genesee of his Seneca people
    whose hunters camped in these hills and valleys,
    returning with their bounty
    where the Genesee flows to its mouth in Ontario.

In the dream
I pick my way down sharp and sliding rocks,
the ochre and amber stain of extraction
lining this bank, to make it to the pool,
like a black hole in its endless depth
but which promises a clear and watery circle
that will carry me back
where I came from.

I rhyme // To see myself, to set the darkness echoing.
from Personal Helicon, Seamus Heaney

I stare down well shafts too, Seamus
and into deep night skies
through the rising breadth of ever-rolling waves,
into the intricacies of leaf-life.

Seeking the shining word-Muse
of my damning craft who rises
hazy, like mirage on a July tarred road.
And, when glimpsed,
her image is made of mirror.

The formula is always the same
the results, miraculously, vary.
Like all dust and sinew of this life
all parts of me careen away from center.
I feel the slow, slack response creeping through my bones,
time tramples crudely across my face,

The words we share alone
are stone-bound
and record this flashing moment.

The kind of poetry I want

is the bald eagle that flushes up in front of me
as I walk through pines and brush along the canal.
He startles me though I expect his presence,
his silent lift stops me as he pulls out and away.

It's my hands jumping out in front of me
at that moment
to grab onto his feathered girth just for a second
because I think no one will believe
how enormous he is and
that I have touched an eagle.

It's my rising heart-rush
when I fail to make contact
But my outstretched hands feel the down sweep of air:
Closer this time.
And the dry, sudden exhale of his wings
beats against my eardrums
a whisper: Next time for sure.

It's his raptor wisdom,
that knows I am coming, knows
he will always win this afternoon game we play.
Knows we will play
anyway.

His Journey

In my dream my father gave me
a small jade rabbit.
It was his way of telling me
that his leaving was real,
a final rite of passage.
There would be no more casual time together
in the way we had known.
This token of closure, a precious stone from the Earth,
on the level of rarity of our sweet, green and earthy bond.

When we are together again, maybe in another dream,
I'll be the eager audience for his stories
of all he's met and done since leaving,
of how the primal love we practice here
makes distance fade to nothing,
how he never left at all.

Young Crow

On the rough grate
fire escape,
your spare remains.
I've seen you there
three weeks now
feathers black
oily and
outspread in
supplication.

I pass and
do not look,
remember the time I stared
saw traces of
wit and game
about your face.

I thought of
the comic magpies
Heckle and Jeckle
from long ago
not like you, really.
They had steady jobs,
actors' union, good
retirement. Benefits.

You flew free and
unencumbered
your whole young life
scavenging the riverbanks
and rooftops.
Now I only want
to scoop up
and cradle
your teacup skull
in my naked palm.

Life is all
about the greed
that swirls around food
and love. What else is there
to fly and die for?

Where Does Creativity Reside in Your Body?

If I say hand or heart or knee or left eye
it oozes past those places—
it cannot be contained.

Like Siddhartha, I see it in my river.
It roams in an unstoppable flow,
life stream that imitates blood,
visits all locations, makes all stops.

It grows in the optic nerve
when I'm eye to eye with canine wisdom,
flits toward the ceiling with the light
from the rotating golden angel Advent candle.

It teases with the tinkle of tiny bells
and the benign murmur of the aging faithful in church.
It's my mother's voice
laughing with the evening light
coming through our kitchen window.

It beckons my nose with salt rising bread in the oven
and the clean sharp scent of pine needles;
directs my fingertips across a warm cotton work shirt,
newly-plucked seashell,
and the memory of the backs of Grandma's hands.

It is the tang of sweet that laces through
my first sip of wine of an evening
and radiates the warmth of peppermint candy
sucked down to a sliver of pale white.

It sleeps in my dreams,
where we dream together.
Boundless, free of my clumsy body,
We take our flight.

When I make the bed

When I make the bed,
I see how my attention to the doing of small things
connects me to the magnitude of my life.
It is in the precision of fitting the corner
of a clean sheet
to the exact curve of the mattress edge
and to tuck it with a skill passed down to me
from grandmothers, aunts and mother.
With care I smooth the cotton twill
then pull it taut in a corner wrap:
making the mattress a gift of comfort
in a snug and ready envelope.

I sweep my hands over the broad treeless plain,
the expanse of white to lie flat
and stay untouched, pristine.
And my life seems more satisfying
when I snap a crisp clean cover over
the carefully and freshly placed sheets,
and watch it float down and settle
unwrinkled and ready to caress
our work-worn bodies with comfort,
with love and promise of sleep.

Fauna in my new yard

Gopher turtles,
black racer snake,
invisible cicadas
slow, silent white egret,
carefully stepping his way through the water.
They scuttle, glide and fly across my mind's eye's stage
preparing for the every-afternoon rain.

In the absence of human interaction,
anole lizards with bright orange dewlaps
step forward to introduce themselves
cicadas drone welcome messages in my sleep.

Humidity eases me down a notch,
releases some vestigial Yankee anxiety.
Not too distant thunder growls over the harbor.

I forgive myself for feeling unsettled and a little lonely,
look for the nine-banded armadillo.

A Stump Ground

It was a Florida white oak,
now a stump that protrudes into our yard.
Below, in the mesh of
the communication network
made of tree roots and mole passageways,
memories of the tree float by quickly
on strands of life like an echo of children playing
in eternal ball fields on summer afternoons
or a muted scent of the cologne
that spoke to me
of ginger and lime.

Ground down
it does not pass.

Its fine, pure existence,
stronger that anything I can be or even conjure,
lives on.
In my melancholy
I reach back to touch it:
the tree, those memories.
I remind myself
that there is something real and wild that lives on here,
rises every morning,
pushes through my veins.

On the Road to the Winn-Dixie

On the road to the Winn-Dixie
I look for the feral pigs I've seen at times
rooting in the roadside brush
black, fat and so damn cute,
they busily push their snouts through the vegetation.

They are not to be seen today.
Maybe they've been routed by
clearing for the next condo complex,
displaced by a dig for sewage lines or swales
or a new road like the one I'm on,
a wilderness way a couple of years ago
now a populated tributary of the nearest highway.

I'm from a place whose ground lost its wildness
centuries ago.
How strange for me to be here to witness
this frantic drive to devour and repurpose.

Like my porcine pals,
I'm pushed to the edge of my familiar existence.
I bury my snout in newly-turned ground
to gain purchase.

And look for roots.

The Alabaster House

(I need the cool outside air.
Need space to expand.
Need my promised land.)

There is a stucco house of alabaster hue
with broad shoulders,
comfortable in its place on a plot
of stolen, sacred land.
There are few told stories
about this land and the souls that passed here.
Just a suburban plot, reclaimed from swamp land,
perhaps unlivable for humans in recent past.
On a web of limestone and dry earth fill
perhaps enough stability for us to squat here
and stay out the remainder of our finger-snap lives.

In the white-washed house
I will dream of what's beneath me
and scan the skies,
wait for visions of native beings
in pampas grass shirts
carrying gopher tortoise shell bowls;
bear thoughts of what's now possible
as this space calls to me to
reach down,
turn over its porous base,
and reveal what is hidden below.

Mary Imo-Stike was born and raised in Rochester, New York.

She worked non-traditional jobs as a railroad track laborer, a plumber, boiler operator and gas line inspector.

Mary received her MFA from West Virginia Wesleyan College in 2015 and served as the poetry co-editor of Heart Wood literary journal.

She was the co-creator of More Than Words* a monthly community literary event in Hurricane, West Virgina. Mary's poems have been published in many journals, one nominated for a Pushcart Prize and her chapbook *In and Out of the Horse Latitudes* was published in 2018 by Finishing Line Press. A longtime resident of West Virginia, she now lives with her husband in Punta Gorda, Florida.

www.ingramcontent.com/pod-product-compliance
Lightning Source LLC
Chambersburg PA
CBHW022104080426
42734CB00009B/1486